Charles Lindbergh

by Lucia Raatma

Compass Point Early Biographies

Content Adviser: Professor Sherry L. Field,
Department of Social Science Education, College of Education,
The University of Georgia

Reading Adviser: Dr. Linda D. Labbo,
Department of Reading Education, College of Education,
The University of Georgia

COMPASS POINT BOOKS

Compass Point Books
3722 West 50th Street, #115
Minneapolis, MN 55410

Visit Compass Point Books on the Internet at *www.compasspointbooks.com* or e-mail your
request to *custserv@compasspointbooks.com*

Photographs ©:

FPG International, cover; Popperfoto/Archive Photos, cover; Index Stock Imagery, 4; FPG International, 6; Museum of
Flight/Corbis, 8; Minnesota Historical Society, 9; Corbis, 10 top; Minnesota Historical Society/John M. Noble, 10 bottom;
Bettmann/Corbis, 13; Corbis, 15; FPG International, 16; Bettmann/Corbis, 17; Archive Photos, 18, 19 top and bottom, 20 top;
Bettmann/Corbis, 20 bottom; FPG International, 21; Bettmann/Corbis, 22; Bernard Gotfryd/Archive Photos, 24; Tom
Nebbia/Corbis, 25; Douglas Peebles/Corbis, 26.

Editors: E. Russell Primm and Emily J. Dolbear
Photo Researcher: Svetlana Zhurkina
Photo Selector: Dawn Friedman
Design: Bradfordesign, Inc.

Library of Congress Cataloging-in-Publication Data

Raatma, Lucia.
    Charles Lindbergh / by Lucia Raatma.
        p. cm. — (Compass Point early biographies)
    Includes bibliographical references and index.
    Summary: A brief biography which focuses on the accomplishments of the first man to fly non-stop
across the Atlantic Ocean.
    ISBN 0-7565-0013-3
        1. Lindbergh, Charles A. (Charles Augustus), 1902–1974—Juvenile literature. 2. Air pilots—
United States—Biography—Juvenile literature. [1. Lindbergh, Charles A. (Charles Augustus),
1902–1974. 2. Air pilots.] I. Title. II. Series.
    TL540.L5 R22 2000
    629.13'092—dc21   00-008636

Table of Contents

A Brave Pilot

Charles Lindbergh was a very brave pilot. He was the first person to fly a plane across the Atlantic Ocean alone and without stopping. Other pilots had flown across the ocean, but they made stops in Newfoundland or Greenland. Charles flew straight from New York City to Paris, France. This flight made him famous.

◀ Charles standing in front of his famous plane, the *Spirit of St. Louis*

Young Charles
with his dog

Early Life

Charles Lindbergh was born on February 4, 1902, in Detroit, Michigan. Back then, no one flew airplanes.

Even as a young man, Charles liked machines. He worked on his family's farm in Minnesota. He liked to fix tractors and drive his father's car. When he was eighteen, Charles left home to go to **college** in Wisconsin. But he found school boring after a few years. He was more interested in flying planes. Airplane flight, or **aviation**, was new. So Charles left college. He entered a flying school in Nebraska.

7

Learning to Fly

Charles learned all he could about flying and planes. He asked his teachers many questions. And he watched the **mechanics** work on the planes.

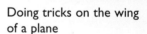

Doing tricks on the wing of a plane

Then Charles became a **barnstormer**. Barnstormers are pilots who do tricks in the air. At that time, barnstormers earned money by performing. Charles put on a good show. He learned how to walk on airplane wings. He made daring jumps with **parachutes**.

But Charles wanted to be a real pilot. When he was twenty-two, he joined the army. He had to work very hard to learn how to fly a plane. When his training was over, Charles was the best pilot in his class.

Charles adjusts his parachute in front of his plane.

Charles was flying mail planes when he heard about a prize for flying across the Atlantic Ocean.

Delivering the Mail

After the army, Charles Lindbergh began working as a pilot carrying mail. In the 1920s, using airplanes to deliver mail was a new idea. It was dangerous work. Many pilots were killed during their flights. Airplanes were not as safe as they are today.

Lindbergh's **airmail route** was from St. Louis, Missouri, to Chicago, Illinois. Sometimes he had to parachute out of his plane. Other times he had to make crash landings. But Charles was a skilled and careful pilot. People could rely on him.

◀ A crashed mail plane piloted by Charles

Making Plans

About this time, a wealthy man named Raymond Orteig offered a prize to the first person to fly across the Atlantic Ocean. The prize was $25,000. Many pilots tried, but they always failed.

Charles Lindbergh felt that he could make the flight if he had the right airplane. Several businessmen in St. Louis gave him money for the project. He designed a plane and had it built. He named it the *Spirit of St. Louis*.

Charles Lindbergh knew the plane had to be very light. A lighter plane would use less fuel. So he did not use anything heavy inside the plane. He had no radio. Instead of a leather pilot's seat, he used a small wicker chair.

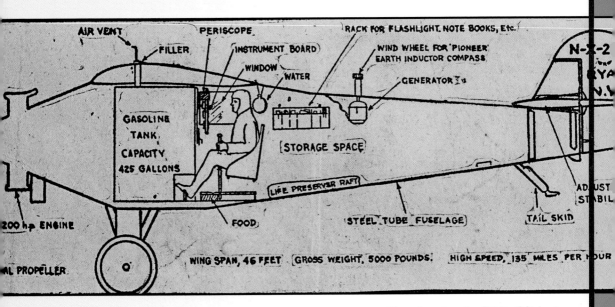

The plans for the *Spirit of St. Louis*

The Famous Flight

Finally, it was time. Charles had tested his plane and planned his route. He was ready.

Charles Lindbergh took off from Roosevelt Field near New York City at 7:52 A.M. on May 20, 1927. During his trip, he flew through storms. And he had to fight to stay awake. He used a small map to help him find his way.

The flight took thirty-three hours. But Charles was successful! He had flown the *Spirit of St. Louis* 3,600 miles (5,792 kilometers)—all the way to Paris. He arrived late at night, but thousands of people greeted him at the airport.

Inspecting the plane before the historic flight ➤

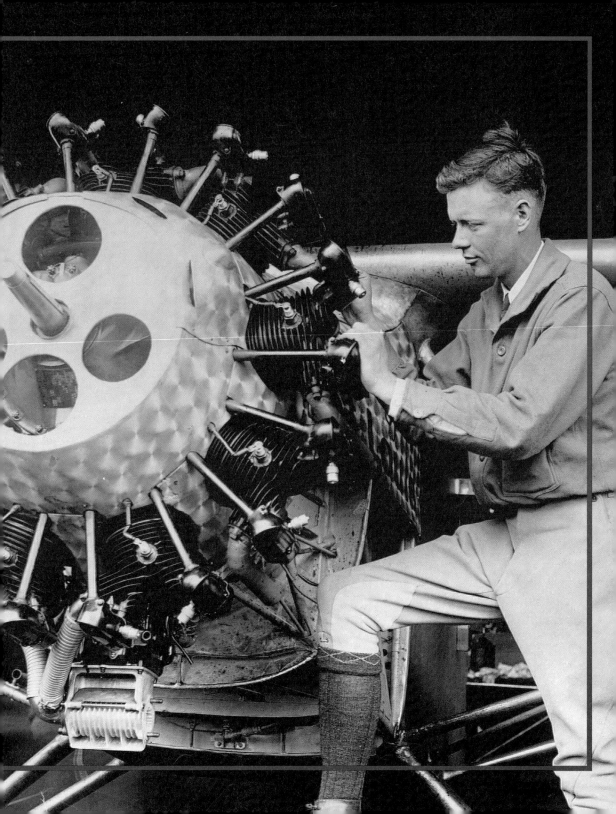

A Hero

Charles Lindbergh
traveled all over
Europe after his
famous flight.
Reporters wanted to

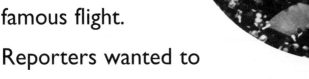

talk to him. Everyone wanted to meet him.

Back in the United States, Charles got a
hero's welcome. He was given parades,
parties, and awards. He told everyone he met
that flying was safe. Charles wanted more
people to fly. He also told airlines how to
build better planes.

Crowds surround the plane in Paris.

Millions of people lined the parade route in New York City

A Family

In 1927, Charles met a young college student
named Anne Morrow on a trip to Mexico.
She was the daughter of the U.S. **ambassador**.
Two years later, Charles and Anne were married.

Charles taught his wife to fly. She went with him on many trips. Together they planned routes around the world for airlines.

Charles and Anne before a flight

Anne and Charles often flew together.

Charles and Anne Lindbergh soon after they married

19

In 1930, they had a son named Charles Jr. Two years later, someone **kidnapped** and killed their son. Newspapers all over the world carried the story. People everywhere shared the sadness of Charles Lindbergh and his wife.

Charles Jr.

Anne with young Charles Jr.

The Lindberghs went on to have five more children. But they never forgot the little boy they had lost. After the death of their son, Charles and Anne traveled to many countries around the world. Charles continued to work

with major airlines. The Lindberghs were glad to be away from the newspaper reporters and sad memories.

Charles and Anne flew to Iceland in 1933.

World War II

During his many travels, Charles Lindbergh visited Germany. The German people and the airplanes he saw there impressed him greatly.

In 1941, the United States entered World War II (1939–1945). Charles Lindbergh felt the United States should stay out of the war. His ideas about Germany and the war made President Franklin D. Roosevelt and other Americans very angry. So Charles was not allowed to serve as an army pilot. Instead, he helped the army improve their planes during the war.

Charles speaking out against World War II

A Hero's End

After World War II, Charles tried to be a more private person. He had never liked being famous.

As a pilot, he had come to love the natural world. So he worked to improve the environment. And he helped save endangered animals.

He also wrote a book called *The Spirit of St. Louis*. It was about his flight from New York to Paris.

Charles Lindbergh

During a trip to the Pacific Islands

In his later years, Charles Lindbergh found out he had cancer. He spent time with his family at his home in Maui, Hawaii. And he thought about the remarkable life he had lived.

On August 26, 1974, the world's most famous pilot died. But his mark on aviation would live forever.

Charles Lindbergh's grave in Hawaii

Important Dates in Charles Lindbergh's Life

1902	Born on February 4 in Detroit, Michigan
1922	Leaves college to study flying in Nebraska; works as a barnstormer
1924	Joins the U.S. Army
1926	Becomes an airmail pilot
1927	Flies the *Spirit of St. Louis* nonstop from New York to Paris
1929	Marries Anne Morrow
1930	Charles Jr. born
1932	Young Charles is kidnapped and killed
1939	Speaks out against U.S. involvement in World War II
1941–1945	Works for aircraft companies
1960s	Supports wildlife conservation
1974	Dies on August 26 in Maui, Hawaii

Glossary

airmail—mail carried by airplane

ambassador—an official representative in a foreign country

aviation—air flight

barnstormer—a pilot who does tricks in the air

college—a place to learn after high school

kidnapped—taken away forcefully

mechanic—a person who fixes machines

parachutes—fabric balloons used to lower people from airplanes

route—direction of travel from one place to another

Did You Know?

- The planes used by airmail pilots were so dangerous that they were called "flaming coffins."

- To keep his plane light for the trip across the Atlantic, Charles Lindbergh cut his maps down to include only the parts he needed.

- Charles Lindbergh was nicknamed "Lucky Lindy."

Want to Know More?

At the Library

Borden, Louise. *Good-bye, Charles Lindbergh: Based on a True Story.* New York: Margaret McElderry, 1998.

Lindbergh, Reeve. *View from the Air: Charles Lindbergh's Earth and Sky.* New York: Puffin, 1996.

Stille, Darlene. *Airplanes.* Danbury, Conn.: Children's Press, 1997.

On the Web

The American Experience: Lindbergh

http://www.pbs.org/wgbh/amex/lindbergh/

For information about the *Lindbergh* PBS film and a timeline for important dates in aviation

The Charles A. and Anne Morrow Lindbergh Foundation

http://www.lindberghfoundation.org/

For information about Lindbergh and useful links

Through the Mail

Federal Aviation Administration

800 Independence Avenue, S.W.

Washington, DC 20591

For information about flying and being a pilot

On the Road

National Air and Space Museum

Seventh and Independence Avenue, S.W.

Washington, DC 20560

202/357-2700

To see the real *Spirit of St. Louis*

Index

About the Author

Lucia Raatma received her bachelor's degree in English literature from the University of South Carolina and her master's degree in cinema studies from New York University. She has written a wide range of books for young people. When she is not researching or writing, she enjoys going to movies, playing tennis, and spending time with her husband, daughter, and golden retriever.